Positive Living

With
Dr. Louis B. Gerhardt
A Tough Minded Optimist

1-800-995-1620   760-367-4627
res19mxc@verizon.net
74007 Playa Vista
Twentynine Palms, CA   92277

Magic Valley Publishers

Sale of this book without a front cover may be unauthorized. If this book is without a cover, it may have been reported to the publisher as "unsold or destroyed" and neither the author nor the publisher may have received payment for it.

    Published by Magic Valley Publishers
    Copyright 2010 © by Dr. Louis B. Gerhardt
    All Rights Reserved.

Except for use in any review, the reproduction of this work in whole or in part in any form by any electronic, mechanical or other means, now known or hereafter invented, including xerography, photocopying and recording, or in any information storage or retrieval system, is forbidden without the written permission of the author through Magic Valley Publishers, 6390 E Willow St, Long Beach, CA 90815 U.S.A.

ISBN 978-0-9845275-2-6

Cover design by Matt Gonzalez
Earth Pledge © 2009 J. Massey, used with permission.
Manufactured in the United States of America

Dedication

Patty Gerhardt, my loyal and strong support as a loving wife and faithful friend.

Grace Gerhardt, my devoted, loving, and patient wife for almost 40 years.

Acknowledgement

Burke Le Sage, a genuine friend.

Maribel Motta and Desiree Musick for always being helpful and considerate.

Judy Massey for her generosity and thoughtfulness.

Preface

Many years ago, a mentor, the late Norman Vincent Peale, wrote a very popular book titled "The Tough Minded Optimist."

I told Dr. Peale in 1965 that if I ever started a newspaper column I intended to call it "Tough Minded Optimism." He thought I had a great idea.

Well, it happened. After 44 years I began writing a column each week for three local newspapers. It has been well accepted by the readers. In addition, it is now appearing in three monthly publications.

I receive good comments almost daily from people who appreciate what I am attempting to accomplish. To put it simply, I want readers to find my columns helpful in their efforts to maintain a positive attitude each day regardless of circumstances.

Now I have written this modest book which is a compilation of what I have written at other times, of what I have spoken in other places, and of how I think and feel about the joyous and challenging circumstances that each of us is experiencing right now in our fascinating lives.

When I write about having a positive attitude, I am not suggesting that people should abandon common sense or deny the reality of extremely difficult situations.

Tough minded optimists are not naïve, Pollyanna-ish, or unrealistic. They recognize the challenge in every difficulty. They are pragmatic, logical, and extremely practical. On the other hand, they have the audacity of hope and a certain belief that something of value may come from any negative experience.

So live in hope, dear friends. Tomorrow will be different. Tomorrow you may hear the music, meet the person, read the book, have the insight, think the thought that changes your life in a beautiful way.

Former Secretary of State Colin Powell is a tough minded optimist. It was Powell who said with deep conviction "perpetual optimism is a force multiplier."

Believe it, my friends, and anticipate with optimism tomorrow, next week, and all your days.

May this plainly written book be a positive aid in every aspect of your life.

Positive Living

Credo

I am a sanguine and debonair pilgrim on a spiritual journey through a fascinating and ever expanding universe. I have come from the heart of God and I will return to God's heart when my traveling days are done.

I selected the adjectives sanguine and debonair with great care. I wanted the words to reflect exactly how I feel.

Sanguine comes to us from the Latin and Middle French and means cheerful, confident, optimistic, up-beat and buoyant. Debonair comes to us from the French and means bearing oneself with personal respect, an always hopeful demeanor, and demonstrating a profound sense of ultimate well-being whatever the circumstances may be at the moment.

In 2007 I offered a lecture in Fresno, California in which I expressed my confidence that the Creator's design for this universe is unfolding as it should and that we should relax and accept the fact that in time all things will work together to serve the Creator's purpose.

My friend of many years, the Rev. Joseph Becker, a Roman Catholic priest, was in the audience and told me later that I was a stoic. Now Father Becker is not only a priest but a university professor so I checked it out. He was right!

I am a stoic in the sense that I agree with Zeno and other early theologians who taught that the Creator will never be defeated by the creatures He created. On the other hand, I go beyond the mind-set of the stoic and I enthusiastically and whole-heartedly think of myself as a Christian. I mean that while I am not interested in a religion ABOUT Jesus I am committed to the teachings OF Jesus. It was Jesus, the Master Teacher, who taught his followers to feed the hungry, cloth the naked, visit the sick, and go to the jail. I suggest you could describe me as a "Christian Stoic."

Some time ago another good friend Derwood Andrews, who has attended many of my lectures, told me that in intellectual matters I was a genuine heretic. Just like Father Becker Derwood instructed me to study the etymology of the word. Derwood was absolutely correct. I am a heretic!

I cannot accept or subscribe to anything that conflicts with my own concept of truth. This means that my theological position has changed through the years and will very likely change again and yet again as I continue to study, think, experience and learn.

My attitude on social and political matters is best described as that of an "activist." It is my belief that the ultimate solution to all social and political problems is an informed, honest, concerned, involved, compassionate and responsible citizenry working within the framework of a free society. Therefore, I believe it to be the primary task of educational and religious institutions to encourage the development of wholly integrated men and women who have a high opinion of themselves, who genuinely respect others, who trust God's creative process, and who nobly and unselfishly strive to so conduct themselves in their individual lives that this world will be a better place because they lived and loved and laughed on this earth.

Only man has the capacity to rise above his physical nature, to be the noble conqueror of himself. Only man, of all the animals of earth, is able to battle the ceaseless demands of the instincts and drives inherent in his nature and subject them to his will. It is true! Man has been created only "a little lower than the angles."

--Louis B. Gerhardt

Trust

Trust is the most important quality we can possess. When I write of trust, I write of an attitude that goes far beyond intellectual formulation to a quiet confidence and an underlying faith in the worthwhileness of life and in the purposefulness of the universe. I write of an attitude based on the thought that God is good and God intends that life should be good. It is the recognition that while life is a continual challenge and there are all kinds of obstacles, we persevere and we overcome because basically we trust. Soren Kierkegaard said that one must come to trust in God as a swimmer comes to trust in the buoyancy of the water. The sea may be 80,000 fathoms deep and the swimmer cannot see the bottom, yet he trusts that he will be buoyed up by the unsinkable buoyancy inherent in the very nature of life itself. This is the quality of trust which produces an attitude by which we can interpret life and the universe in such a way that, despite all the sorrows of this life, we are able to commit ourselves in confidence and faith.

During the great depression in the early 30's our family lived on a "stump ranch" in the mountains of Western Washington. We had no electricity, no in-door plumbing, and barely enough food. It was rough. On Sunday mornings, at the ages of five, six, and seven my younger brother, my cousin and I would walk down the railroad tracks that ran through our property to a little country church that met in White Horse School. We learned a hymn there which has affected my outlook on life to this day. The words went something like this:

> "Simply trusting every day,
> Trusting all along life's way,
> Even when my faith is small,
> Simply trusting that is all."

Werhner Van Braun, the brilliant rocket scientist put it like this: "All I have seen in this life encourages me to trust all that I have not seen."

An Excerpt from "Desiderata"

You are a child of the universe no less than the trees and the stars; you have a right to be here. And whether or not it is clear to you, no doubt the universe is unfolding as it should. Therefore be at peace with God, whatever you conceive Him to be. And whatever your labors and aspirations, in the noisy confusion of life, keep peace in your soul. With all its sham, drudgery and broken dreams, it is still a beautiful world.

--Max Ehrmann

***

These words have been of much help to me through the years. Ehrmann died in 1945, but when I served our church in Terre Haute, Indiana 1963-67, I often walked by his former home and recalled his beautiful thoughts and comforting works. I memorized the words on this page and often quoted them to myself and others. Adlai Stevenson, the former governor of Illinois and Ambassador to the United Nations who died in 1965 planned to print and distribute Ehrmann's prose and poetry as Christmas gifts that year.

Confidence

I have an unwavering confidence with an underlying trust that God is good beyond our dreams, that the facts of life are friendly, that the things of the universe are meant to work in harmony with the things of the spirit, and that God's purpose will never finally be defeated by the creatures He creates. I believe that in the end we will all share in the accomplishment of God's desire and it will be marvelous to our eyes.

--Louis B. Gerhardt

Look To This Day

In 1936, at the age of eleven, I stayed home from school because I had the flu. My parents brought the family radio into the bedroom for my enjoyment. I heard an announcer on KXRO, Aberdeen, Washington read something I never forgot. It made such an impression on my fertile mind that I memorized it and have been helped by it ever since.

It is from the Sanskrit, the language of Ancient India, and it was written more than 4,000 years ago.

> Look to this day!
> For it is life, the very life of life.
> In its brief course lie all the verities and
> realities of your existence;
> The bliss of growth;

> The glory of action;
> The splendor of beauty;
> For yesterday is already a dream,
> and tomorrow is only a vision;
> But today, well lived, makes every
> yesterday a dream of happiness,
> and every
> tomorrow a vision of hope.
> Look well, therefore, to this day!

That perceptive philosopher of long ago was right on! Actually it could have been written in 2010.

Learn to live in "day-tight compartments." The Bible wisely suggests, "Do not be anxious about tomorrow, today's own troubles are sufficient for the day." The Latin phrase is "carpe diem" and it means "seize the day." And when we do this—when we enter and leave each day with the proper attitude of mind—we live better lives. An unknown poet has written:

> The day will bring some lovely thing,"
> I say it over each new dawn;
> Some gay, adventurous thing to hold
> Against my heart when it is gone.
> And so I rise and go to meet
> The day with wings upon my feet.
> I come upon it unaware-
> Some sudden beauty without name;
> A snatch of song—a breath of pine—
> A poem lit with golden flame;
> High-tangled bird notes—keenly thinned—
> Like flying color on the wing.
>
> No day has ever failed me quite—
> Before the grayest day is done,

> I come upon some misty bloom
> Or a late line of crimson sun.
> Each night I pause—remembering
> Some gay, adventurous, lovely thing.

With such an attitude you can possess the day. To whom am I writing? I am writing to the person who is wrestling with the problem of drugs, alcohol, sexual frustration or any other of the difficulties encountered in this life. *You can make it through to night fall!* Don't borrow tomorrow's troubles today. You can't have tomorrow's strength until tomorrow, so don't burden yourself with what might happen then. And remember this: Every day that a problem is conquered makes it more likely that the problem can be conquered for good. The psychological and physical rewards of a victorious day will make you a more robust fighter in the day that lies ahead. It is the happier person who has learned to take life a day at a time. I feel so sorry for people who can never enjoy the moment because of the regrets of yesterday or the fears of tomorrow.

I like the way former president George W. Bush put it in a speech in Fort Worth, Texas some nine months after leaving office. "I can tell you some days were great, some days not so great! But every day was joyous."

That's it! Discover the satisfaction and joys that are to be found in each and every day.

Delivering a lecture in 2006.

The Power of Love

For many years I have been sharing my personal definition of love with all those in attendance at my seminars. I tell them that love is the sincere desire to do what you genuinely believe is in the best interest of the object of your love. It's as simple and challenging as that.

Love is the most powerful force ever experienced by mankind. In ways far beyond our present understanding love accomplishes miracle after miracle and continues to give us hope even when all seems lost.

In the mid-60's a professor at John Hopkins University gave a group of graduate students this assignment:

"Go to [name withheld] slum area. Identify 200 boys who live there and are between the ages of 12 and 16, get a profile on their family situations and backgrounds. Then predict what is likely for their respective futures."

The graduate students found the boys and did the interviews, gathered additional data, and examined the social statistics for the area. They concluded that 90 percent of the boys would spend time in jail or prison.

Twenty-five years later another group of graduate students was given the assignment of testing that prediction. Some of the boys—now men—still lived in the area, a few had died, and a few others couldn't be located. Amazingly, they made contact with 180 of the 200.

Only four of them had ever been incarcerated. Since the area was now even more a breeding place for crime, the researchers were intrigued. Those who ventured to explain kept saying, "Well, there was this teacher..." Checking further, they discovered that three fourths of the 180 had been taught by the same woman.

They located her in a retirement facility and asked her how she had exerted such an influence on these boys, that is, could she explain why she loomed so large in their past and their memories.

"No," she said, "I really have no idea." She was quiet for several moments. Then she said musingly—

more to herself than to her interviewers: "I did so love those boys…"

The Child Within You

There is a little child within you and if you are wise you will heed the child.

The child is the intuitive sensitive self, incongruously remaining young inside an aging body, never quite accepting what logic says is real and true.

Too much, I think, do we lean on the counsel of the surface self that has grown in worldly wisdom through the years – the cynical, ingrown self that neither trusts nor ventures, that fears new things, that dares not to be foolish and thus truly sane in a world that is cautious, sophisticated and insane.

C.J. Jung says all of this better and more fully than I can, but this I can do, I can counsel you not to abuse the child within – the child which is the innocent you – by neglect or disavowal. The vulnerable, poetic, life-renewing child within you is always there if you will but take time to play with him. He endures, though you neglect him, and he is with you to the end.

Not Then and Not Tomorrow

During my time as editor of *The Congregationalist*, I received a large number of articles, stories, and poems from always hopeful and often anxious writers.

The most unforgettable experience I had in that regard began with a submission I received from Francis Maguire of New York City in the fall of 1976. It was a brief poem. I liked it very much and I decided to buy it. I wrote to Mr. Maguire and, after congratulating him on his poem, informed him that he would receive a check when the poem was published.

He wrote back requesting immediate payment because his landlord was pressuring him. I sent him a check by return mail. Two weeks later the check was returned and stamped across the envelope was the word: DECEASED. I went ahead with my plan to publish the poem. It appeared on the back cover of the magazine surrounded by appropriate artwork. It was well received. It read:

> *You spend your life*
> *preparing yourself*
> *for what never happens.*
> *And then you say,*
> *"Oh, dear, I missed it."*
> *Was it ….Then?"*
> *Oh, no, not then.*
> *And not tomorrow.*
> *Between.*

Miracle

I listen
With sensitivity of heart
To the Voice of Life;
I hear
The persistent invitation,
"Enjoy! Enjoy!"

I listen
With awareness of mind
To the Voice of Life;
I hear
The insistent whisper,
"Now! The time is now!"

        I respond
        With openness of soul
        To the Voice of Life;
        I experience
        What is most beautiful—
        The miracle of now!
                --Louis B. Gerhardt

You Are Unique

"Know thyself" is one of the wisest statements ever uttered. Who said it first is open to debate. Plutarch gives the credit to Plato. Others have ascribed it to Pythagoras. Still others say Socrates and some suggest Solon. Actually, it doesn't really matter. The important thing is for us to recognize and accept the validity of this basic wisdom. Only then can we become wholly integrated men and women.

Centuries later Shakespeare wrote "to thine own self be true" and I believe that this powerful statement logically follows after the cogent statement to "know thyself."

If we are to accomplish this, however, we must gladly recognize, accept, and even revel in our freedom to do so. Yes, dear friends, we are free to become the men and women that in our very best moments we really want to be. I repeat we all have the capability to be psychologically free.

It is strictly up to us. It is our own decision. We are free. Glory in your freedom!

And now to the most wonderful thing of all. You are unique. There is no one in all the universe like you. Rejoice in your uniqueness.

One of America's finest writers was William Saroyan and I have been "hooked" on his writing since I read "The Time of Your Life" in 1940 at the age of 15. In fact, I carried his books with me to war and read and reread them by flashlight in my zipped-up sleeping bag on the front lines of France, Belgium, Holland, and Germany.

I was delighted, therefore, when I read that one of Saroyan's friends once remarked to him that Saroyan was a genius. Saroyan immediately answered, "of course I'm a genius. There is no one in the world like me. You cannot become like me."

This revealing anecdote leads me to the following personal comments which I hope will bring us to the sum of this brief essay.

Sometimes when I read the writings of a Tolstoy or a Dostoevsky I wish I could write as powerfully and as beautifully as they. Some-times when I listen to the words of a Martin Luther

King, Jr. or a Winston Churchill I wish I could speak as eloquently and persuasively as they.

Most of the time, however, I know better than to entertain such disquieting thoughts. Most of the time I am quite content to simply be me and to recognize in other people interesting variations of myself.

Each of us is unique, and through the years I have found joy in discovering that aspect of uniqueness that makes you supremely you and me supremely me.

I take delight in believing with the psalmist that each of us is "fearfully and wonderfully made."

It seems to me, therefore, that a significant step toward the building of a peaceful world is to be found in glorifying the uniqueness, beauty, and integrity of each person, especially our very own self.

Father Ian Hanley and Lou planning positive living seminars for the two Episcopal churches of the Hi Desert during 2008.

Peace

I believe that an indescribable peace is experienced deep within the soul of a person when they recognize the uniqueness of their life and their relationship to all creation, their unity with the universe and all its powers; when they realize that at the center of the universe dwells the Creator of all things, and that this center is really everywhere, especially within their very own self.

--Louis B. Gerhardt

The Saving Remnant

As we read of the shenanigans, the ear marks, the pork barrel projects, and the machinations of lobbyists and politicians, many of us become cynical. Some of us are tempted to declare "Every man has his price." This pessimistic and negative attitude bothers me and so I offer you a more positive perspective.

In the early years of the 18th century, Sir Robert Walpole, first earl of Oxford, was reputed to have told a colleague that he knew the price of every man in the House of Commons.

A shortened version of his alleged comment has come down to us as the familiar statement: "Every man has his price."

The truth of the matter, however, is that Walpole did not say that at all.

What he actually said was "I know the price of every man in this House except three." That is the truth of the matter. That is the glory of it all.

Do not lose heart, my friends. There has always been and there will always be the "saving remnant."

It has been my happy experience through the years to recognize in every profession, every trade, every aspect of business and in every institution, strong men and women of such impeccable character, such decency of mind, such unflinching courage, and, dare I write it, such simple goodness that in time even the most grievous situations have been alleviated.

Those of you who are reading this small book will be interested in learning that when I first wrote this anecdote about Sir Walpole and had it printed in my weekly column I was approached by a man I admire very much, Ken Hansen, a former reporter for the Los Angeles Times, who questioned my illustration concerning Sir Walpole and told me that he had searched everywhere and found no facts to back up my story. Well, that really bothered me because I couldn't remember where I got that information. All I knew for certain was that I hadn't made it up.

Finally, in intellectual desperation, I turned to my long-time associate Burke Le Sage who has thousands of books, dictionaries, encyclopedias, etc. and asked for his help. He couldn't find the collaboration I needed either; not even with the help of his wife Jean Bixby on her computer.

Then Burke got a bright idea and he and his friend Don Korhonen went to the Copper Mountain College library and asked student worker Eddie Ruiz for assistance. And Eddie found it!

The May 11, 1907 "Notes and Queries," printed in London, quotes Sir Wolpole as declaring to a Mr. Levenson "I know the price of every man in this House except three and one of them is your brother, Lord Cower."

Thanks to Burke, Don, and Eddie I was able to assure Ken and others that my fact was correct even when I couldn't remember my source.

My Best Man Was Gay

When Patty and I had our church wedding in 1995 our dear friend, the late Paul Isner, was my best man. Paul was an openly gay person. He had a high opinion of himself and lived his relatively brief life with dignity and enthusiasm.

I first met Paul while I was serving as Senior Minister of First Congregational Church in metropolitan Los Angeles. The church building is magnificent and houses the largest church pipe organ in the world. Many people congregate there daily for noon organ concerts and to participate in other church activities. Paul was one of those people. He also enjoyed visiting our home in South Pasadena.

With my late wife, Grace, and our son Loren I moved to Fresno in 1980 to serve our church there. Shortly after our arrival Paul wrote and asked if he could come to Fresno, live with us, and work at the church. We welcomed him and he immediately became the church organist and worked in the church office. Many months later Paul went to San Diego to work in the city's superior library system and to play the organ for a large Christian Science church in the Greater San Diego area.

Paul physically died in 2005 and I conducted his memorial service in San Diego's downtown branch library. I then conducted another memorial service and commitment at the Crystal Cathedral in Garden Grove. He was only 42 and died unexpectedly of "natural causes."

I share all this with you because my late wife Grace (he was the organist at her funeral) and my wife Patty loved him very much and we learned so much from him and his friends about the wonderful men and women who make up the LGBT community. In fact, Mike Lipsitz, editor of a very influential LGBT newsletter in the Hi-Desert and beyond is a close personal friend, supporter, and advisor on my non-profit projects.

Therefore, I believe I am able to write with some authority on the subject of homosexuality. I have been a minister and counselor for better than 55 years and I have been in constructive and caring relationships with gay people all over the country. I have officiated at the weddings of many gay couples and have had many gay people on the boards and committees of the churches I have served.

The purpose of all I have written, of course, is to make it absolutely clear that I deplore attempts by some misguided, usually religiously oriented, people to portray homosexuals as men and women who are simply "sick" or "abnormal," who could be cured of their "sinful" ways if they just determined to do so. Believe me, that kind of superficial thinking is just plain wrong, wrong, wrong.

In 1973 the American Psychiatric Association issued a strong statement stating that homosexuality is not a mental disorder. I strongly maintain that and men and women live more wholesome and happier lives when they accept without misgivings who and what they are.

In 1979 Mayor Thomas Bradley and the City of Los Angeles presented me with a Certificate of Appreciation for 25 years of effort to bring together different races, religions, and ethnic groups in a genuine spirit of mutual respect. I am pleased that I received that recognition.

Now I pray and work for a day when all people regardless of sexual orientation have all the rights, privileges and genuine respect often reserved for heterosexuals.

48

A Letter to the Editor
Printed in Time Magazine--2006

In 1963 you selected Dr. Martin Luther King, Jr. as "Man of the Year." In 1964 he was awarded the Nobel Peace Prize. He was a man of superior intelligence, an extra-ordinary leader and a passionate crusader for total justice for all people everywhere. We observe a national holiday in his honor.

It grieves me deeply, therefore, that you felt it necessary to place him on the cover of the January 9 issue and print material that can only diminish his stature among his admirers and embolden many of his detractors.

I am not disputing the material in the article I am only lamenting the fact that so many people seem to find it necessary to expose the "clay feet" of our heroes.

Some would respond by saying, "Let's be real," but I see the deterioration of something very precious in the human community.

The Rev. Louis Gerhardt, D.D.
Twenty-nine Palms, CA

Process

    I believe we are made in the likeness of God and are in the process (this very moment!) of becoming our true selves. I believe this process is a ceaseless one and that it continues on and on beyond out present understanding. I mean that there is absolutely no limit to the potentialities of people. Whatever is imagined in a person's mind and desired in a person's heart can be achieved. The primary requirement is that we trust God's creative process. Each of us must trust the worthwhileness of life and the goodness of every living thing – especially our very own selves.

    ---Louis B. Gerhardt

Patience

You cannot control a child's life. A child will go where it will go. You can only stand patiently and wait. A child will go to where the excitement is and then it will return to where it has known love.

--Louis B. Gerhardt

The Family and Its Future

Don't you believe it! The American family is NOT about to lose its position as the basic unit of society. In fact, it is my contention that we are participating in a period of increasingly rapid social change during which both the precious intimacy and mutual sharing of family life are becoming more and more appreciated by the people of our society. As a result, I predict *a recovery of family life in the next twenty five years that will provide the basic foundation for an improved social order.*

I am aware that there are many people with a different point of view. These alarmists have historical precedents, reams of statistics, the pessimistic pronouncements of eminent sociologists and the dire forecasts of gloomy theologians to support the contention that the family is in widespread decay. These people insist that there is little hope of anyone really doing very much about the situation and they suggest that the most constructive thing we can do is get our spiritual house in order and, despairing of this life, prepare as best we can for "the life beyond."

I don't accept this negative outlook. I believe the factors usually cited as being the most contributory to the dissolution of the family are, in reality, the very factors that are shaping new patterns of family life! I also believe that the "new family pattern" brought on by these changes will prove as precious to those who share them as were the family experiences we nostalgically recall from our younger days.

Among the many factors which I feel are helping to form the family of the future, three in particular are worth noting:

1. *The reality of "the lonely crowd."*

Ironically, this era, marked by the need "to belong," and containing the greatest number of groups in social history to which one can belong, is also the era marked by a growing sense of personal isolation. The more groups one joins, the less he or she really belongs to any. And people desperately need to *belong!*

Carson McCullers dramatically illustrates this truth in her novel "Member of the Wedding" in which a 12 year old girl is described in the throes of adolescence. She is particularly upset by the necessity of adjusting to the impending wedding of her brother. Thinking of him with his girl and what it will be like when they are married, the little girl suddenly feels left out. She is alone and her feelings are summed up in the author's words: "They are them and in Winter Hill together, while she was her and in the same old town all by herself….She was an *I* person….all the other people had a *we* to claim, all other except her."

Everybody needs to belong in the deepest sense of a *we*. In the simple language of heartbreaking childhood, McCullers has fathomed this powerful and supreme truth about life. We *do* have to belong to a *we* before we can truly live. And Man is experiencing the truth of that!

Man is becoming very much aware that his deepest emotional needs are NOT being met by joining more organizations and participating in more social clubs. He is literally returning home. He is rediscovering the family. He is realizing that only in the comfort, affection, reassurance, forgiveness and acceptance of his loved ones can these emotional needs be fulfilled. It was Gibson Winters, noted sociologist, who wrote of the family as "the exclusive sphere of intimacy in modern life." He was convinced that the family is the last bastion of *meaningful personal relationships* in our society. And "the lonely crowd" is becoming convinced as well.

2. The *"fourth-dimensional woman."*

We have been reading and hearing much in recent years about a new concept of the role of women in our society. There is an insistence by more and more women that they be emancipated from any restrictions imposed simply by the fact of their sex or because of society's stereotyped notions of what constitutes a good wife and mother. And, glory be, women ARE being emancipated! They are becoming more and more involved in social organizations, political activities, cultural pursuits and recreational interests. More wives and mothers are enjoying greater freedom to develop to their full capacity in all aspects of life than ever before.

Some people think of this liberation as detrimental to the best interests of the family. I do not. I am convinced that the eventual results will provide more wholesome and happy family situations. In Dr. A. W. Maslow's "Motivation and Research" we read that "Capacities clamor to be used, and cease their clamor only when they are well used. That is, capacities are also needs. Not only is it fun to use our capacities, but it is also necessary." Traditionally, women were not encouraged, or expected, to use their full capacities. In fact, as Betty Frieden suggested in her revolutionary book "The Feminine Mystique," women, in the name of femininity, were encouraged to evade human growth.

Today, however, the situation is vastly different, and I believe this new development will result in more integrated family units. Why? Because surely, two people, who have the opportunity to grow and develop freely and to maintain their individuality while lavishly expressing their deep love and concern for each other, are more likely to create that environment of respect for human personality so essential to the raising of well-integrated children and the maintenance of a happy family. This spirit of togetherness without loss of individuality is conveyed in the words of Kahlil Gibran: "let there be spaces in your togetherness…stand together yet not too near together: For the pillars of the temple stand apart, and the oak tree and the cypress grow not in each other's shadow."

3. *The increasing mobility of the population.*

Frequently family shifting from one place to another is cited as a factor in the obvious disarray in society today. However, even the experience of moving can have its beneficial aspects. Faced with a bewildering succession of strange environments, the father, mother and children find in their familiar family relationships a reassuring oasis of "the known" in the desert of the unknown. Thus, mobility, instead of driving a family apart can, in fact, result in increased family cohesion, bringing a new appreciation of the importance and blessedness of the familiar and dependable love and understanding found only in the continuing stability of the family relationship.

There are many more factors indicating that the future of the American family is bright. Suffice to note that this essay seeks only to substantiate and encourage a positive attitude, a spirit of optimism and the recognition that the family will ultimately prevail over all the factors tending to destroy it.

Even Bishops Can Be Wrong

In 1870, a bishop was visiting a small denominational college in Oberlin, Ohio. He expressed to the president of the college that nothing new could be invented. The educator disagreed and said, 'Why, in 50 years, I believe it may be possible to soar through the air like birds.' The shocked bishop responded, 'Flight is reserved strictly for the angels, and I beg you not to repeat your suggestion lest you be guilty of blasphemy!'

That bishop was none other than Milton Wright, the father of Orville and Wilbur.

Any religion that professes to be concerned about the souls of men and is not concerned about the slums that dam them, the economic conditions that strangle them, and the social conditions that cripple them is a spiritually moribund religion awaiting burial.

--Harry Emerson Fosdick

Friendship

When my son, Loren, died unexpectedly several years ago our friends immediately rallied to our support. We received a large number of telephone calls, e-mails, cards, letters, and flowers from friends all over the country. In addition our friends here in the Hi-Desert, including the local clergy, surrounded my wife Patty, and me with genuine concern and much love. We will always re-member the many expressions of sympathy and acts of kindness offered without hesitation by our friends.

These many acts of friendship set me to thinking about the use of the word friend, the high claim of friendship, and what it means to have a friend or to be a friend. That is, a genuine friend. I mean a man or woman who is totally loyal to you regardless of any conceivable situation.

The Bible states that "A friend loves at all times" (Proverbs 17:17) and "A friend sticks closer than a brother" (Proverbs 18:24).

Believe me, a sincere friend is extremely rare. It was Shakespeare who wrote, "A friend should bear his friend's infirmities." How true! Yet, you are most fortunate, indeed, if you have even one friend who will bear your moral, mental, emotional or physical infirmities.

On a personal basis, I am blessed with several such friends. I have both men and women friends who will "go to the wall" for me. The matter, however, is far larger than that. The question is whether or not, should the occasion arise, I will "go to the wall" for them.

Friendship, you see, is a two-way street. Emerson wrote, "The only way to have a friend is to be one." And I believe it.

It was precisely what Jesus had in mind when he said, "You are my friends, if you do what I ask of you" (John 15:14).

When a person earnestly sings "What a friend we have in Jesus," I often wonder if the singer asks "Does Jesus have a friend in me?"

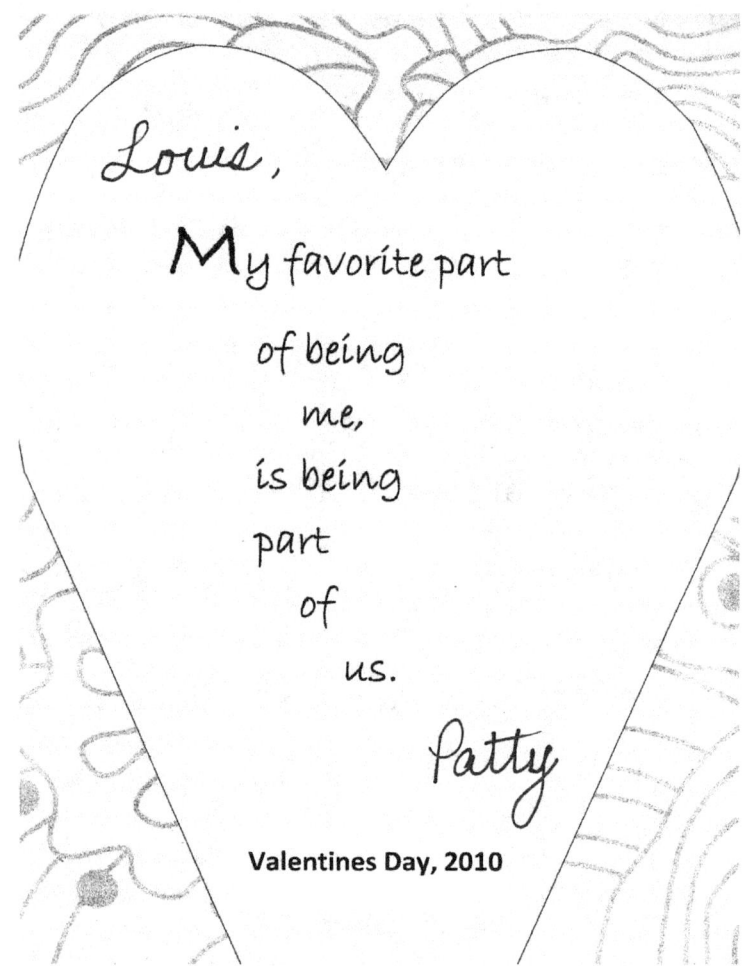

Louis,

My favorite part of being me, is being part of us.

Patty

Valentines Day, 2010

Love Without Reservation

Love without reservation,

Love unquestionably

Greener grass doesn't abound.

Nurture what you have,

Cherish the moments.

Encapsulate the beginning,

Bottle it, refill annually

Place on the altar,

Worship always.

Never forsake it,

Remember the best

Forget the rest

Life's short.

Love without reservation.
                    --Herman Platzke

"I Decline to Accept the End of Man"

I decline to accept the end of man. It is easy enough to say that man is immortal simply because he will endure; that when the last ding-dong of doom has clanged and faded from the last worthless rock hanging tideless in the last red and dying evening, that even then there will still be one more sound: that of his puny, inexhaustible voice, still talking.

I refuse to accept this. I believe that man will not merely endure: he will prevail. He is immortal, not because he alone among creatures has an inexhaustible voice but because he has a soul, a spirit capable of compassion and sacrifice and endurance.

--William Faulkner
In acceptance of Nobel Prize Award, 1950

The Fairest Gifts

It is an obvious fact that for the most part we inherited the world in which we live. We had nothing to say about the kind of a world into which we were born. The world was here a long time before we arrived and the world was given to us at birth. It was given to us as it was made and developed and as it has grown through the centuries. The categories of thought were given to us. The nature of our bodies was given to us. The language that we inherit and use for our expression and development of thought was given to us. The customs and traditions which determine so much of what we like or dislike were given to us. And as we grow older we realize our impotence to change it very much.

We feel a great deal of the time that we are complete victims of the forces that move around us and through us. It is this, of course, which leads so many people to talk about everything being determined; that there is no such thing as freedom.

But this is only one part of the total complex. You can proceed to take entirely the opposite approach to this whole matter if you wish. I see this given world, for example, through *my* eyes, not yours. The world I live in is *my* world. *I* made it! I is *my* way of seeing that determines the world in which I live. I do not see your world. I do not feel your world. I do not understand things the way you understand them. The things that I find beautiful might be ugly to you. The things that are sometimes so transcendently important to me are passed by many times by my friends who do not see what I see.

The world that each one of us has is a private world. Each of us determines the things that he sees. Each of us determines his reactions to the experiences of life. Each of us judges and decides the validity and the quality of his friends, his neighbors, the events of the world. It is our own individual system of values that determines those things to which we pay attention. And each person creates his own system. You are not forced to see the world the way another person does. It is not necessary that that person who I think is a good person be a good person in your opinion. You don't have to love the people that you, yourself, have chosen to love. They are your choice. They are your decision. They comprise and illustrate and reflect the kind of world that you are making or have made for yourself.

Now nothing can be really understood—and we cannot properly evaluate ourselves and our problems or our world—unless we understand and we really appreciate the fact that the world we live in is our world and that we made it. A quotation from Vincinzcey's book, *Rules of Chaos*, states:

"In literature, as in life, the meaning and reality of any act cannot be given—only taken." This is essentially the same important and basic truth that I have been describing. In support of Mr. Vincinzcey, please note that when a good artist describes an event in the life of one of his characters, he never gives you the interpretation. He never tells you what it means. He never explains it.

I was in Chicago some years ago and observed Edward Albee being interviewed on a television program. The interviewer kept trying to get Edward Albee to explain his plays and to delineate what they were attempting to say. Albee refused, saying, "It's up to the audience to determine what my plays mean and what they say. That is their choice. That is their decision."

And so it is that two reviewers can see one of Kurt Schauppner's fine plays or films and one can write that it was poor and another can write that it was marvelous! It is always true that what any artist's creation conveys is dependent upon the kinds of values the observers have chosen, the kinds of worlds in which the observers live. And so two of us, looking at exactly the same event, can come out with totally different understandings of the nature of the event, the meaning of the event, the thing that caused the event, the results of the event. Actually, they may be two totally different events in the eyes of two interested observers.

I repeat, each of us is living in a world he has made. Thus, for us to understand each other we have to somehow or other comprehend the nature and the quality of the world in which the other person lives. Unless we do that, we violate him and he will violate us if he does not understand that we have our own system, our own style, our own understanding and our own values.

So, for a better understanding of ourselves and our young people today, we must ask what world do they live in? And by what standard do we judge them? Our horror and dismay over how they see our world is misplaced. For they do not see our world! They have seen their own world and it isn't our world. They have not been given what we thought we had given them because they did not take it. You cannot really give another person an interpretation of your world. You cannot give another person your understanding, or your appreciation, or your courage or your strength. How dismayed we are over and over again when we have tried so desperately to give our children or our friends something precious and beautiful to us—something beyond all value—and they haven't seen it! They didn't even hear what we said! You can't give another person the meaning and the significance of the events in their life…or yours. They will take what they want to take. They will take what they are able to take. And they will create their own world in their own way.

That is why effective counseling takes so long. In counseling the good counselor is not the person who says, "I'm going to give you my insight, my courage, my ideas; I'm going to help you to see it my way." The good psychologist, the good counselor, is the person who, over weeks and weeks and months and months, helps people to see themselves and their world in a wholesome way so that they accept themselves and the world they have been given with an affirmative attitude. That is why we need trained and professional counselors. You see, we should not be trying to give people what we have. Rather we should try to help men and women find within themselves what they already have and to help them understand themselves and others in a more creative way. That's why people come seeking help...they think they lack something...but they don't really lack anything. They just haven't found themselves and accepted themselves and, even more important, learned how to apply their real selves to their real world.

During the many years I served local churches, people would often come to me and say, "You've been such a help to me." And I would get so many cards and letters that have notes in them that read. "Oh, you've been such a help to me." Sometimes they would come from complete strangers or at least from people I didn't really know. And I would feel like protesting, "I'm not even aware of your name!" But deep inside I already know what the reply would be, "Oh, that doesn't matter…you've still been a help to me."

Why did people say I helped them? I insist it is not because I gave something to a person; rather, it is because that person took from me what he or she wanted. They took from the service what they wanted. They took from the music what they wanted. They took from the prayer what they needed. You see, we can't give to the worshipper; the worshipper has to take. We can't give courage. We can't give understanding. We can't give confidence. We can't give hope. The worshipper must take those things. We can't give faith; the worshipper must take it! We can't give the belief in the child Jesus who, so filled with the love of God, was God with us transforming lives. We can't give that belief; that belief must be taken!

This is the dramatic meaning for me in that incident in the life of Jesus when the woman reached out and touched the hem of Jesus' garment and was healed. She stretched forth her hand in trust and took from Jesus. That's what makes it the powerful story that it is…that she reached out in trust and took!

It happens to us over and over again. Someone is so meaningful to me and they don't even know it. I take from them. They have something I want and I take it. And so it is with our friends who deal with us. And so it is with our children. And so it is with our parents and with society. If there is a lesson that comes through loud and clear to me as I live in this life, it is that perhaps we should not try so hard to give to other people what we think is important and valuable. It seems to me that the more we try to give, the less our loved ones are able to take. Perhaps we ought not to be so concerned with giving our children the things that we think are important. Perhaps we ought not to try to give them our religion, our standards, our understanding, our appreciations, our values or our world...for, in truth, we cannot really give those things.

What then can we give? Thornton Wilder expressed it well in *The Eighth Day:* "The fairest gifts are those of which the donor is unconscious. They are conveyed over the years in the innumerable occasions of daily life...in glance, pause, jest, smile, expression of admiration or disapproval. The fairest gifts are the gifts we give of ourselves, and they are the most rare."

May we be the unconscious donors who give the fairest gifts and thus encourage those we love to reach out into this life to take for themselves their very own world.

Sister Joseph Grace of St. Vincent Medical Center, Orville Kelly, author of "Make Today Count", Lou, and Rabbi Bernard Cohen, noted ecumenical speaker participate in the 1979 Interfaith Thanksgiving Service at First Congregational Church, Los Angeles, Dr. Louis Gerhardt, Senior Minister.

The Ecumenical Spirit

When Chelsea Clinton and Marc Mezvinsky were married by a Jewish chaplain at Yale and a Methodist minister, July 31, 2010, we were reminded that ecumenicity in the United States is for real. The fact is that more than 37 percent of all weddings in this country are inter-faith marriages. This is a wholesome development.

When Grace, my wife of almost 40 years, died in 1994 our dear friend Rabbi Bernard Cohen officiated at her memorial services along with a Roman Catholic priest and a Protestant minister. When Patty and I were married in 1995 the same rabbi, priest, and minister officiated.

I believe there is nothing more significant in positive cultural development than people of different philosophies respecting and loving one another.

It is my sincere belief that someday the spirit of ecumenism will dominate the world and "nation will not rise against nation and men will not make war anymore."

It almost goes without the need of comment that you and I must be ferocious fighters against prejudice in any form, however subtle.

Marcel Proust wrote, "The universe is true for all of us and different for each of us."

Perhaps that is the way it should be.

An ancient Hebrew prayer puts it very well:

"From the cowardice that shrinks from new truth, From the laziness that is content with half-truths, From the arrogance that thinks it knows all truth, Oh, God of truth, deliver us."

Now it happens that much of what you have read in this brief essay appeared in my weekly newpaper column shortly after the Clinton-Mezvinsky wedding took place. A reader e-mailed almost immediately to strongly advise me I was championing a point of view that would "water down" Christianity and lead toward the creation of a new world church which he claimed has already begun.

Well, I think that is absurd. I believe you can be totally committed and even extremely vocal about your particular theology and still be a person who has a spirit of solidarity with all humankind and respects (not tolerates) every person of the universe.

My spirit is that of John Wesley, founder of the Methodist Church, who wrote:

Give me thine hand! I do not mean, be of my opinion; you need not. I do not expect or desire it, neither do I mean I will be of your opinion...Keep your opinion and I mine, as steadily as ever.

You need not endeavor to come over to me, or to bring over to you. I do not desire to dispute points or to hear or speak one word concerning them. Only give me thine hand!

I do not mean embrace my modes or worship, or I will embrace yours. I have no desire to dispute with you one moment; let all matters stand aside, let them never come into sight.

If thine heart is as my heart, if thou love God and all mankind, I ask no more, give me thine hand.

Lou rings the bells in the winter of 1996 in front of the Adobe Market in Twentynine Palms.

In the winter of 1944 Lou fought as an infantry soldier in the Battle of the Bulge. The Salvation Army was there.

When God Is Born

Whenever a person
   Is helped from darkness
And begins finding beauty
   In his life;

Whenever a person
   Is lifted from despair
And begins finding joy
   In her life;

Whenever a person
   Is rescued from emptiness
And begins finding meaning
   In their life,

God is being born.
        --Louis B. Gerhardt

My friend George Gullen of Wayne University, Detroit went to visit a family in need, and on leaving the home, one of the sons admired the new car George was driving. George told the boy that the car had been given to him by his brother. The boy would be expected to reply "I wish I had a brother like that!" But, rather, he said, "I wish I could be a brother like that!"

The Value of Humor

I am an early riser and I start the day, seven days a week, reading three daily newspapers—The Los Angeles Times, The San Bernardino Sun and The Desert Sun.

I always begin by reading the comics. I don't read every strip or cartoon but I read all the funny ones. My favorites include Blondie, Peanuts, Beetle Bailey, Family Circus, Dennis the Menace, and Hazel. I also enjoy the clever cartoons in our two local weeklies, especially those drawn weekly by Tim O'Connor for The Desert Trail, Twentynine Palms, California.

Reading humorous cartoons is not only a delightful habit but it also increases a person's life span. Serious studies from the University of Wisconsin reveals that people who read the comics before the obituaries have markedly longer life spans. It makes sense to me!

A sense of humor is a powerful attribute that can do much to improve the health and well-being of any person who makes the concerted effort to develop this inherent gift from the Creator.

That's one of the reasons I never miss the daily newscasts on radio Z 107.7 FM. Gary Daigneault and Les Taylor always provide a joke for the morning and other light-hearted banter that gets my day off to a good start.

No less an authority than the renowned theologian Reinhold Niebuhr led me to believe that humor and laughter are both basic to the development of a truly satisfying religious life. It was Dr. Niebuhr who wrote, "Humor is a prelude to faith and laughter is the beginning of prayer. Pass it on!" Well, I have spent a lifetime living the advice of my brilliant contemporary and passing it on. I have always kept humor and genuine laughter at the heart of all I say and do.

You may recall the Bible story that describes how God told the 100 year old Abraham and the 91 year old Sarah that they would have a child. Both of them laughed.

How ridiculous an idea! Yet a year later a son was born. They named him Isaac which means laughter.

I believe God has a sense of humor and he wants you to have one too. I believe a laugh-a-day helps keep the doctor away.

UCLA has released the results of a study, which validates all I have said in the past about the significance of humor and laughter in achieving and/or maintaining good health. Working with men and women at Loma Linda University, UCLA researchers were able to document that even the anticipation of a funny event changed mood states which, in turn, triggered profound positive physiological changes in the body.

Moreover, the leader of the test Dr. Lee Berk reported that the mood change lasts well after the event itself, supporting the reality that an optimistic state of mind can enable people to overcome pessimism and doubt and face the future with confidence and hope.

Here are a few tips you may want to consider:

1) Be sociable. People in groups laugh 30 times more often than people who are alone.
2) Start your day with humor. Read the comics in the newspaper. Listen to a funny disc jockey on your way to work.
3) Share a joke that made you laugh when you heard it. If it's good you'll laugh again when you tell it to someone else. (Shortly before this book went to press a long time loyal friend, Lu Ella Mees, telephoned to

read me a joke from a magazine. We laughed together and we hung up. That's what I'm writing about.)

4) Smile. It's easier to laugh when you have a head start.

The psalmist, bless him, put it into a theological framework. He wrote in Psalm 126, "When the Lord restored the fortunes of Zion, we were like those who dream. Then our mouth was filled with laughter and our tongue with shouts of joy."

So, laugh dear friends. You'll feel better, others will feel better and somehow, I think God likes that.

I Stand by the Door

I stand by the door.
I neither go too far in, nor stay too far our,
The door is the most important door in the world—
It is the door through which men walk when they find God.
There's no use my going way inside, and staying there,
When so many are still outside and they, as much as I,
Crave to know where the door is.
And all that so many ever find
Is only the wall where a door ought to be.
They creep along the wall like blind men,
With outstretched, groping hands;
Feeling for a door, knowing there must be a door,
Yet they never find it...
              So I stand by the door.
                  --Samuel Shoemaker

The root of the matter is a very simple, old-fashioned thing, a thing so simple I am almost ashamed to mention it, for fear of the derisive smile with which wise cynics will greet my words. The thing I mean—please forgive me for mentioning it—is love—Christian love. If you feel this, you have a motive for existence, a guide in action, a reason for courage, an imperative necessity for intellectual honesty.

--Bertrand Russell

What About The Right To Die?

One of the most challenging problems in the medical care field is the rising cost of taking care of people in what is called the "end-stage" phase of life. The "end-stage" phase is the last phase of the life of a terminally ill person. It may come as a startling fact that over sixty five percent of all money spent in the field of medical care is spent on people who are not only terminally ill but are in the last six months of their life span!

Now, the implications of this are enormous as we think of a society in which more and more people are living longer; in which more and more people are over seventy years of age. In the state of California alone there are six and one half million people over seventy years of age and the number grows daily. Therefore, we have a growing number of people in the "end stage" phase of life and the medical costs continue to rise.

This situation has resulted in well intentioned, compassionate and professionally competent nursing home personnel, medical doctors and hospital staffs dealing more and more with the question of to what extent life support systems should be used to keep alive the patients under their care.

Some years ago then Governor Richard Lamm of Colorado, a brilliant and thoughtful man, spoke to the Colorado Health Association and said something that reverberated across the country. He said that we have a duty to die and to get out of the way with all of our machines and all of our artificial hearts. Well, you can imagine the uproar! Some people got the idea that Governor Lamm was saying that older people were simply a problem to be eliminated. But he was not saying that at all. What he was saying was that something has got to be done. We are living a society in which scientific achievement is such that we are already able to keep human tissue alive in bodies that for all practical purposes are no more than human vegetables. Governor Richard Lamm was simply asking what we are going to do about it. Who is going to draw the line? How are we going to decide the monstrous moral and ethical issues at stake? It is not a simple matter, it is a burgeoning problem. It is an issue with which we must deal.

It is difficult, isn't it? I know it is for me. And I know that in the theological, medical and legal worlds there is considerable chaos and a great deal of confusion.

Legally as you know, the confusion ranges all the way from legal authorities on one side saying a person has not only the rights of life, liberty and the pursuit of happiness but also the right to decide how they are going to die; to the other side of the legal question, that claims every single avenue available must be used to maintain and support the continuance of life in the human body.

There are medical people on the one side who feel compulsively unwilling to stop at anything to keep body functions technically alive and there are medical people on the other side of the question who are perfectly willing to pull the plug. In fact, the late Dr. Denton Cooley, the man credited with installing the first artificial heart in a human being, put it like this: "I have pulled the plug many times in life support situations. While relatively few medical people seem willing to do this, I have done it. Clergy, relatives, and others should be consulted but the decision to terminate life support efforts should be made by doctors. Doctors should shoulder the responsibility. I have pulled the plug. In fact, in my hospital I feel responsible for making such decisions and I make them the most careful way I can." It has obviously sneaked up on us, hasn't it?

Like a great many other parts of life together, the scientific world, the technical experts have outstripped our moral and ethical means to handle new inventions, new discoveries, new methods. As a moral issue, it is a new issue. You don't directly find this problem in the Bible.

In Biblical times life expectancy was about thirty years of age. Disease and malnutrition and filth were the order of the day and what passed as medical advice and treatment was just as likely to kill you as to heal you. Therefore our current moral and ethical problem was of little concern to them. In fact very little is said in the Bible about anything of this nature but you can look in the Book of Common Prayer in the Church of England and you will find a prayer that contains this line "from sudden death, O Lord, deliver us" but I suspect that in this day and age there are many people who would like to rewrite that prayer and have it say "from a living death, that is neither alive, nor quite dead, good Lord from that, deliver us."

It really is not so much a moral or legal issue as it is a spiritual issue, a very personal spiritual issue. The subject is not so much how we are going to deal with death, but what is life, what really is life? What is life and what is not? Jesus said in the scriptures "I have come to bring **life**, life in all fullness, life in abundance." What is life?" When does a person cease to any longer be a person and only become a medical achievement? What reasonable responsibilities will we accept and what decisions will we make about that time when our bodies and minds are no longer capable of really maintaining and experiencing the abundant life? What are the conditions under which we will stop at nothing to hang onto our own bodies and the bodies of those we love, and the conditions under which we will allow them to return to the God from Whom we came?

If you are like me you wince at the very thought of actual decision making taking place at that level. Yet one thing is quite clear. You and I, living when we do and where we do, do not have the luxury of those who went before us; the luxury of not thinking about this, the luxury of not developing some working understanding and personal maturity that helps us to make the kind of decisions that are now being required in the world in which we live.

You see, this is a terribly complex and terribly personal matter. Probably it has to remain that way but we have lives to live, we have decisions to make, and as we move ahead in this rapidly expanding technological revolution we have to develop ethical and theological answers to these questions.

Now, there are two "red herrings" which I want to mention and then we can cast them aside and not let them bother us in the decision making process. One of them, one of these "red herrings," that needs to be purged from the discussion, is a very ponderous, very loaded term. It is the one that speaks of "playing God." More often than not it is intoned as a kind of "coup de grace," the ultimate "conversation stopper," and it is supposed to send us scurrying with our tails between our legs back into some kind of mindless passivity. Someone will remind us with a kind of "stained-glass" voice, "How dare you play God." Well, that just isn't the unanswerable question that it is cracked up to be. If playing God means what it is obviously intended to mean, that is making awesome decisions that affect our lives, the quality of our lives, the direction in which we are going as a people, we do it every day. We do it every day, and we do it with regularity. How can I put it more bluntly? We play God every time we interfere with the apparent course of events, the random process of things. We play God every time we decide to have a baby. We play

God when we go ahead and have our appendix out and not let a nice, natural, ordinary case of peritonitis do us in. We play God every time we hire a policeman, give him a gun and send him out on a dark street to deal with crime. We play God when we dam up a river, when we cut down a forest and when we dig into the ground and mine the coal. We play God every day of our lives. That's not an issue. When someone says to you as you are making a decision "You are playing God!" they are talking nonsense and trying to keep you from living up to the responsibilities that are yours as a son or daughter of God.

The other "red herring" that is sometimes brought up in discussions of this nature has to do with the commandment, "Thou shalt not kill."

When all other medical and legal considerations are resolved, if they ever are finally resolved, there is still going to be this persistent, haunting word in our ear, "Thou shalt not kill! Thou shalt not kill! Thou shalt not disconnect the kidney machine! Thou shalt not pull the plug. You are destroying life. You are killing!"

In 1973 Orval Kelly, a dear friend of mine formed the organization "Make Today Count" in Burlington, Iowa. Some time later we were visiting Black Hawk Tech, a nursing school in Wisconsin, and while speaking to the students, Kelly asked the question, "Do you believe that medical personnel should be permitted to cease providing life support activities for a hopelessly ill person? In other words, should medical personnel be permitted to pull the plug?" Every student in both classes, morning and afternoon, raised their hand acknowledging that they believed medical personnel should have that kind of power and decision making control over the body. Then Kelly asked the question, "Who, here, is willing to pull the plug?" In the morning classes, which consisted of about one hundred and fifty students, not one person raised their hand; and in the afternoon class we had only one potential nurse who raised her hand. It is an awesome question, isn't it? Who is will to pull the plug? Deep in the psyche of all of us, are those haunting words, "Thou shalt not kill."

Therefore, for the purpose of this discussion, a proper interpretation of this very important commandment is required. We must realize that what the commandment actually means is "Thou shalt not murder." We are not to take the life of another out of jealousy, out of personal conflict, or out of convenience. Obviously, this commandment does not apply to the question that faces us as a society in this brief essay.

What are we going to do about terminally ill people in the technological world in which we live today? A group of medical doctors in New England got together and published, in the New England Journal of Medicine, an excellent article which they call "The Bill of Rights For Dying Patients and Their Families." These prominent medical doctors in this marvelous medical journal are suggesting that we have simply got to develop guidelines for people to follow as they experience this decision making process in their lives. Among the points they state are these: (a) Patients need to know, they have the right to know, that they are in the dying process. (b) The family needs to know and has a right to know. (c) Families and patients need to be free to determine whether or not they want life support systems. (d) Doctors should not be made to feel guilty or be open to libel because they remove life support systems.

May I suggest if we really believe in eternal life, let us not cling to the hopelessly ill but allow them to go and be with the God who gave them life. We find it written in the book of Ecclesiastes, "To every thing there is a season and a time to every purpose under the heavens. There is a time to be born and a time to die. God has set eternity in the hearts of men and God has made everything beautiful in its time."

The great Indian chief Cochise, maybe the most philosophical of all the warrior chiefs, said "Every man has a time to die; no man should outlive his time." There is profound wisdom in that.

One of my contemporary heroes was Senator Frank Church of Idaho. Frank Church was, in my judgement, an extremely able and gifted man. He gave so much to this country. He learned he was terminally ill some months ago and that he would soon die. Senator Church said, "I want to go home, I want to go home to die." He went home and just two weeks ago last Sunday he ate his last meal with his family and then returned to his bed. As the days went by, his friends and relatives came to visit with him. Senator George McGovern came to see him. By then Frank Church only weighed about a hundred pounds, and George McGovern picked Senator Church up in his arms, held him close, and he kissed him and said, "I love you, Frank." And then, as Senator McGovern laid Frank Church back in bed, Frank whispered, "You are a dear, dear man, George." Then Senator Edward Kennedy came and for two days Senator Kennedy sat at the bedside of Frank Church. Frank could not talk anymore but that was all right. Ed Kennedy just held his hand, told Frank what his contributions meant to us all, shared anecdotes with him and people could tell by the look in Frank's eyes that he understood and enjoyed what Kennedy had to say. Then, on the day before Church died, his daughter-in-law flew down from Boston. She came into his bedroom, crawled up on the bed, and laid herself down beside Senator Church. Senator Church's wife laid herself down at his other side. They touched him and they kissed him, and they held him close. They spent the night just lying there together and as it neared morning the daughter-in-law left the room. Now just the husband and the wife lay together.

Later their son reported that as the first gray shafts of early dawn came streaming through the window, Senator Church died and his soul returned to the God who gave him life.

That's the way to die, allowing death to take place in the goodness of God's time. What about the right to die? Let no one take it from us.

There is something more important than physical life. It is the ongoing life of the spirit. With our physical death comes a release of that spirit to a loving God.

Kelly's Prayer

"Father...

Give me the strength to face each night before the dawn

Give me the courage to watch my children at play and my

wife at my side without a trace of sorrow in my smile;

Let me count each passing moment, as I once marked the

fleeting days and nights;

And give me hope for each tomorrow.

Let my dreams be dreams of the future.

But when my life on earth is over, let there be no sadness,

                                                --Orville Kelly

My Prescription For Sorrow

We have always recognized that the pain of deep sorrow is one of the most excruciating forms of suffering a person can endure. We also know that it is a natural pain and that the healing power lies within the wound itself. One of the wonders of our minds and bodies is that while scars remain, wounds *do* heal. This is especially true of sorrow. I am confident that when you experience the agony of grief in your life, you will not only endure it but you will prevail over it and once again know peace of mind and experience the joy and excitement of living. You think I exaggerate? No, it *will* happen to you. But, of course, it will happen much more quickly and permanently if, in the days of relative tranquility, you anticipate the inevitability of grief by developing a constructive attitude toward it. Thus, I suggest to you my own prescription for sorrow—a prescription that has been of immense help to me and could be of significant help to you.

My prescription for sorrow has four parts.

1. Accept the certainty of sorrow in your life.
2. Allow others to share your grief.
3. Live a day at a time with the confidence that tomorrow will be different.
4. Use your experience of sorrow for the healing of others.

1. Accept the certainty of sorrow in your life. Jesus said, "In the world you

have tribulation." In the world you will experience disappointment, loneliness, tragedy and loss. You will suffer. It is inevitable. It is one of the "givens" of life. There is no place in the Bible where you are promised that even the most sincere commitments and the most sacrificial efforts will be rewarded with an escape from grief. You *will* suffer! We *all* will suffer. This I know. I have suffered; even now I hurt. I had a son Loren, who physically died very unexpectedly at age 39, and a loyal and loving wife, Grace, who physically died after almost 40 years of marriage. And if you have not truly grieved—you will. There is no escape.

Consequently, the wise religious leaders are those who are thoughtful enough, honest enough and courageous enough to make this fundamental and poignant truth abundantly clear. Sorrow *does* come to all. It comes to the just and to the unjust, to the righteous and to the evil, to the wise and to the foolish. Sorrow is no respecter of persons. You would think that recognition of this obvious fact would eliminate such irrational questions as "Why is this happening to me? And "What did I ever do to deserve this?"; but it does not. I can only hope that these words will help to accomplish that.

Actually, the experience of sorrow has a positive side! Edwin Markham wrote:

Defeat may serve as well as victory

To shake the soul and let the glory out.

When the great oak is straining in the wind,

The boughs drink in new beauty and the trunk

Sends down a deeper root on the windward side.

Only the soul that knows the mighty grief

Can know the mighty rapture. Sorrows come

To stretch out spaces in the heart for joy.

It seems ordained that life is so designed that no one reaches the promised land without going through the wilderness. Thus, I urge you to recognize now the certainty of personal sorrow and to accept it without bitterness or resentment.

2. Allow others to share your grief. You have concerned friends and understanding relatives who want to help you. As a result of my own experience, which includes 55 years as an ordained minister, I can testify to you that I have never witnessed a time of tragedy or heartbreak but that spiritual giants and beautiful people made themselves available—often to the point of personal risk and self-sacrifice—to voluntarily minister to the need. Please don't be hesitant about sharing your grief with the *right person.* Just be careful to select a listener who has a robust outlook on life and a confident trust in the overall purposes of God. And

when you share your sorrow, express yourself without restraint.

In Ecclesiastes are these quaint words, "By sadness of countenance the heart is made glad." The ancient peoples knew that the release of emotion during times of sorrow was wholesome but we are more likely to consider it good form to repress, conceal and even deny our natural feelings of grief. This is wrong. Open and honest evidence of sorrow is both normal and beneficial. If you want to cry, then cry. Tears are not a sign of weakness or a lack of faith. God in his compassion has given us the merciful release of tears. Jesus wept openly and without shame. There is therapeutic value in the release of tears.

Despite the fact that Mohammed taught the unmurmuring acceptance of whatever life may bring us, it is told that when Seid, Mohammed's closest personal associate, died, Seid's daughter came upon Mohammed, broken and in tears. When in bewilderment she asked, "What do I see?", he answered with moving simplicity, "You see a friend weeping over his friend." A person can stand great sorrow and loss provided the emotions are not bottled up. There is a wise psychology behind the practice of confession—and I do not mean the confession of sin only but the confession of grief. Shakespeare wrote:

"Give sorrow words; the grief that does not speak,
Whispers the o'er-fraught heart, and bids it break."

3. Live a day at a time with the confidence that tomorrow will be different. Learn to live in "day-tight compartments." The Bible wisely suggests, "Do not be anxious about tomorrow, today's own troubles are sufficient for the day." The Latin phrase is "carpe diem" and it means "seize the day." And when you do this—when you confront your sorrow and your grief a day at a time—you *will* overcome! Don't borrow tomorrow's sorrow today. You can't have tomorrow's strength until tomorrow, so don't worry about what might happen then. And remember this: Every day that passes makes it more likely that your sorrow will be conquered for good. The psychological and physical rewards of a victorious day will make you a stronger person in the day that lies

ahead. It is the happier person who has learned to take life a day at a time in sweet anticipation of a wholesome change occurring as the days go by.

I believe that if you face each day with your total strength (regardless of how little strength you seem to have), almost imperceptibly constructive changes do occur and the day comes when life is good again. When, in your anguish and pain you cry, "How long, O Lord, how long," if you listen, you will hear the response, "Weeping may tarry for the night, but joy cometh in the morning." Remember, my friends, the darkness passes, but what one learns in the darkness remains with one forever.

4. Use your experience of sorrow for the healing of others. You have

something very special to offer others in their own hours of grief—something countless people will not yet be in a position to give—an understanding based on a shared experience. Therefore, don't shy away from an opportunity to help when it arises because you don't feel capable of handling the situation. Your own experience of deep sorrow will be qualification enough if you offer it in a spirit of sympathy and compassion. Normally, of course, you should wait until the post-graduate phase of your sorrow. You should be careful to allow enough time to pass following your own experience of grief to be certain that you *will* be a genuine strength to another person. You may be assured, however, that when you do have confidence in your own emotional stability, you will be the most effective support a person going through a similar experience can possibly know.

An Experience I'll Never Forget

I began my first full-time pastorate in 1955 in a small city located in eastern Washington just south of the Canadian border. A few weeks after my arrival the incident occurred that I share with you. I wrote about it in 1967 for the "The Congregationalist," our denominational magazine.

***

It was a good day for a funeral, as funeral days go, with a few rays of sun filtering into the church. Standing in the choir room waiting to begin my first funeral service as pastor of the First Congregational Church of Chewelah, Washington, I hoped that those few rays represented a few rays of hope too.

Funerals are major events in a small town, and Chewelah was no exception. The three marriages I had performed and the several appropriately satisfactory Sunday morning sermons I had delivered had given me the comfortable feeling that I was almost, if not completely, accepted by my congregation, but the ultimate test of my professional ability was about to occur with my first funeral as Pastor.

Until this moment I had been confident that I would meet the challenge when it came. But suddenly, in this silent room, as I sat watching dust particles dance in the sunlight, I was experiencing an anxiety attack. I had no notion of how I could get through this funeral and maintain my favorable position with my flock gathering in the next room, considering the information I had collected about the deceased.

The sound of the phone ringing brought me out of my panic, and as I collected my wits I debated the wisdom of answering it. It was just such an unexpected call only four days ago that had thrown me into this situation. I had hurried to answer the phone then, now I was not so sure I even wanted to respond to it. The ringing of the phone sent back to the call that had dominated my life for the past few days. I remembered hearing the voice of the local funeral director on the other end of the phone.

Augie Martin's familiar voice was saying, "Lou? I've got a job for you." Augie proceeded to tell me about a farmer from east of town who had walked out into a stubble field that morning and blown himself to bits with a stick of dynamite.

"Not one of my parishioners...?" I asked with a sinking heart.

"My gosh, no. I wouldn't break it to you this way if it were somebody important," he said. My own relief was so great that I let that odd remark go by without commenting — but wondered how he could say any person wasn't "important." The man's name was Earl Witham, Augie went on, and he hadn't been the church-going type.

"Then why call me?"

"Oh, I just thought it was time you preached a funeral sermon," he answered. With that brief telephone conversation I became involved in the life and times of Earl Witham. An unknown, a stranger was to be my special challenge, my first funeral in Chewelah. And, as a minister of a small town church, I would be expected to preach a most respectful and respectable funeral oration. City sermons full of generalizations and familiar scriptures simply wouldn't work here, where everyone knows everything about everybody for six generations back. A good, hometown funeral sermon had to be an honest attempt to evaluate the final significance of the deceased person's life. Otherwise the minister is judged a failure.

Perhaps this wasn't such a bad yardstick. A good local pastor ought to be able to sum up the meaning of a man's life in twenty minutes. Yet, delivering the eulogy for some poor suicide victim, especially Earl Witham, was hardly the kind of test I had anticipated in Chewelah.

I remember how after Augie had hung up, my first move was to go out and try to find out who this fellow was, and what had brought him to this sad end. His wife would know him best, but Augie had indicated to me that she was in the hospital and could not be told about her husband's death. There was no other family. I would have to talk to the people who had done business with him: his neighbors, his friends, anyone who knew him in any way.

Augie had mentioned something about Earl being a farmer. Surely Herman Brown, the feed store owner, could talk to me about him.

"Yeah, he used to trade here," Herman told me. "Mean old coot – and not so old at that I guess. Maybe 50, 55 at most. Seemed like he always needed a shave and a bath, if you know what I mean." Herman went on to tell me that Earl never had much to say, but when he did it was likely to be disagreeable. He had run up a bill at the feed store, never paid it, and Herman had threatened to take him to court. After Herman cut off his credit Earl quit going to the feed store.

I was feeling a little sorry for Earl Witham now. There's always a little bad in the best of men, and plenty of decent people don't know how to behave when they're confronted with money problems. Witham might simply have been embarrassed because he couldn't pay his feed bill. Even so, Herman's financial loss was hardly food for Earl's funeral service.

Just outside the feed store I ran into young Doc Hammerberg and asked him if he had time for a cup of coffee. He took me up on the offer, which gave me a chance to ask him if he had known the deceased. Doc hadn't known the man personally but he had heard of him. The news of the suicide had been all over the hospital that morning and out of curiosity he had asked about Mrs. Witham's condition. He had learned that she had a possible fractured skull, a broken wrist, some missing teeth, and perhaps internal bleeding.

As Doc told the story, it sounded as if surely Mrs. Witham had been seriously injured in an automobile accident – yet, rumor had it that her injuries were the result of a fight with her husband two nights ago – a fight which ended when Witham picked her up and threw her bodily out of a second story window. A man on the road had realized she was badly hurt and called an ambulance. He told the attendants that she had jumped, but, as Doc pointed out "What grown woman, even a suicidal one, would jump through a *closed window?*"

By the time Doc and I finished our coffee I was really dismayed by the task in front of me. I had always believed that there is good in every man, but my hope of finding it in Earl was slowly dwindling. And John Gerrish, the coffee shop owner, didn't ease my worry with his own stories of Earl brawling in Chewelah's only tavern. Gerrish sheepishly admitted to liking a beer now and then, and he said "I go down there to the tavern maybe once a week." He said that Witham came in only once in a while too, but when he did he drank as if his life depended on that cheap whiskey — drinking it straight down, one shot after another, until most men would have been unconscious. "Then he'd get mean and, often as not, pick a fight. He didn't fight fair either," Gerrish remarked. "One time I saw him cut up a guy with a broken bottle."

Gerrish's stories were ugly. And all the other stories I had heard, and was about to hear, were just as bad. There seemed no way around the fact that Earl Witham had been an ugly man.

It was mid-afternoon on the second day, twenty four hours before the service, when I remembered Art Jethro, a neighbor of Witham's. He had reported the suicide. Even better for me, Jethro was a deacon in my church. Surely, living so close to the Withams, he would know the good in the man, if anyone would. Art would be honest and understand my position, that I represented not only myself but my entire church when I rose to sum up the life of Earl Witham.

Art was at home and he took me over to see the Witham place. There wasn't much to see, but what there was dovetailed with what I'd heard. The front yard was mostly bare, packed earth with a few tufts of grass bravely rooted in the desolate ground. The house needed painting badly, and Art pointed to one of the many broken windows, saying that was the one Mrs. Witham had gone through.

As I slowly scanned the place, all I could see was accumulated junk in the back yard, a broken roofed barn, and the smell of despair and desolation all around.

Art wasn't saying much, though. He was a quiet, somewhat serious man and watching him, I realized I had never heard him speak ill of anyone. He believed in looking on the bright side of things, in his own solemn way. Art was the ideal man to help me find the good qualities of his deceased neighbor. He could strengthen and reaffirm my tottering faith in the essential goodness of all men.

But he didn't. He was saying, "I don't like to speak ill of the dead, Reverend, but Earl Witham was bad clear through. Most any day or night we could hear him screaming at his wife. He was a bad man and the worst neighbor I ever had."

Finally, I stopped at the hospital to see and talk to Mrs. Witham. Between the bandages and bruises and the obvious concern of those taking care of her, I sensed the futility of trying to learn anything from Mrs. Witham that would change the picture. Earl's widow was in no condition to speak to me. As I stood by her doorway, a feeling of utter defeat crept through my being. Earl was going to be my undoing, too.

Far into the night before the funeral I read my Bible, prayed, and thought. Nothing came to me. Not only was I grappling with a eulogy for Earl, but also my own sense of shock at not being able to find one good thing about the man and what that meant to me personally. I had hoped to get acquainted with this dead man and find the beautiful parts of his life through his friends, only to learn that he had no friends. He had made himself completely unlikable. He had not a single redeeming virtue, and apparently all who came in contact with him would have been better off had they never met, or had Earl never lived at all.

And now, only minutes before the service must begin, the phone in the study was ringing. Trying to ignore it, I cautiously peered out at the assembling crowd through a crack in the door and saw that my worst fears were being realized. Just as I had suspected, the more bizarre the death, the greater the attendance. Earl may have had no friends, but he had a full house for his last rites. People were crowded into the vestibule and no doubt there were others lined up outside. Oddly enough, on the front pew, sat the Steven County Sheriff and every one of his deputies. Why?

The phone kept ringing. With only a few minutes to go, soon I would have to face this anxious and somewhat mixed crowd. There were familiar faces, new faces, and that strange, quiet block of uniformed, sober men in the front row. Why?

On a sudden impulse I fled to the back study and answered the phone. The operator was saying, "This is a long distance call for the Reverend Louis Gerhardt."

"This is he speaking."

There was a short delay and the sound of coins in a pay phone. Then a man's voice asked, "Rev Gerhardt? This is Joe Zulianski in Spokane. I read in the papers this morning about Mr. Witham and I want to come to Chewelah. I can't make the service in time but I'm at the airport now and I can meet you at the cemetery. Can you tell me what one it is?"

I told him and added, "If you're a relative I can hold the service for you. There's no other family present."

"No, I'm not a relative but Earl Witham was better than a father to me. He was the finest man who ever lived." I was speechless. Recovering my composure, I asked, "This may sound strange to you Mr. Zulianski, but could you tell me briefly why you thought so much of Mr. Witham? It's very important."

"Just a minute," he replied. Then he spoke to someone at his end of the line. "I have only a few minutes," he said, returning to our conversation, "but I'll try."

"Three years ago I was about six weeks from drinking myself to death. I had malnutrition from putting nothing in my mouth less than 90 proof, and that was all I cared about." Joe went on to explain how he had been picked up by the Chewelah police and charged with being drunk and disorderly. He couldn't remember how he had gotten to such a backwater town in the first place, but he ended up in the Stevens County jail. That was when he had met Ear Witham.

"He used to drop by the jail and talk to the Sheriff," Joe was saying. "When I dried out he talked to me. He told me many times that he knew how it was to have trouble and he'd like to help me get back on track. The Sheriff told me that Mr. Witham did that kind of thing all the time. You might say he was a one man Salvation Army for the guys he took under his wing." (I thought of that front pew.)

Witham had visited Zulinski regularly; bringing him little things like a deck of cards, a magazine, or a candy bar. When Joe was released, Witham had taken him home – home to that rundown old house next to Art Jethro's.

"He fattened me up and talked a lot of sense to me, and he wouldn't let me get within smellin' distance of a bottle," the voice on the other end was saying. "When I could look at him with clear eyes and without shaking, Mr. Witham brought me up to Spokane and helped me find a job."

When he finished, I found myself struggling for words. I was overwhelmed. I was clenching the phone so hard that my hand was sweaty and my ear was numb from holding the earpiece so closely. For a moment Joe said no more, then he added "Oh, yes, maybe you'd like to know that I got married last year, and there'll be a little one in the house I a few months. You know, Reverend Gerhardt, I'd be in Potter's field if it weren't for Mr. Earl Witham."

I was a tumult of emotions. On the one hand, I felt vindicated. There is good in every man if you look hard enough. And I felt sad that Earl was able to give so much to others, but couldn't give that same respect, belief and goodness to himself and those around him. I believe his wife saw it, and that may have contributed to her staying. I hoped so...I prayed so.

I knew now what I was going to say to the people waiting for me in the church sanctuary. Time teaches us all that life is messy, and it's complicated. And so it's arrogant for us to assume we know another human being based on actions alone.

I told them that we are all important – one way or another, sometimes in an obvious way to everyone, sometimes in ways known only to a very few, but always known by God. And sometimes, someone like Earl Witham comes along, and everyone is sure he was just plain ugly, without any redeeming qualities. But today, on this fine day for a funeral, Earl Witham would leave this earth teaching us all something about ourselves and our judgments.

I also reminded them that we honor God when we feed the hungry, give water to the thirsty, provide shelter for the stranger, give clothing to the naked, visit the sick, and go to the jail to help the prisoners.

***

Looking back over the 56 years since Earl Witham's funeral and considering other experiences that have occurred in my life I still have no rational answer as to why seemingly good people behave the ugly way they sometimes do. I read about horrific atrocities being committed in widely disparate places in this world by men and women of every conceivable background and ethnicity and I remain just as baffled as the so-called "experts" do.

In the midst of her incredible suffering during the Second World War the 14 year old Anne Frank wrote in her diary "It is really a wonder that I haven't dropped all my ideals, because they seem so absurd and impossible to carry out. Yet I keep them in spite of everything because I believe that people are really good at heart."

Love is Real and Life is Sweet

www.ingramcontent.com/pod-product-compliance
Lightning Source LLC
Chambersburg PA
CBHW051437290426
44109CB00016B/1593